Summer

meditations

JOHN BARTUNEK, LC, SThD

Liguori

Imprimi Potest:
Stephen T. Rehrauer, CSsR, Provincial
Denver Province, the Redemptorists

Imprimi Potest:
Fr. John Connor, LC, Territorial Director
Territory of Northern America, Legionaries of Christ

Published by Liguori Publications
Liguori, Missouri 63057

To order, visit Liguori.org or call 800-325-9521.

Library of Congress Cataloging-in-Publication Data

Names: Bartunek, John, author.
Title: Summer meditations / John Bartunek, LC, SThD
Description: First Edition. | Liguori : Liguori Publications, 2016.
Identifiers: LCCN 2016003002 (print) | LCCN 2016005157 (ebook)
         ISBN 978-0-7648-2562-0 | ISBN 978-0-7648-7013-2 ()
Subjects: LCSH: Summer—Religious aspects—Christianity—Meditations.
    Spiritual exercises.
Classification: LCC BV135.S96 B37 2016 (print) | LCC BV135.S96 (ebook) /' DDC
    242—dc23
LC record available at http://lccn.loc.gov/2016003002

Liguori Publications, a nonprofit corporation, is an apostolate of the Redemptorists. To learn more about the Redemptorists, visit Redemptorists.com.

Printed in the United States of America

20 19 18 17 16 / 5 4 3 2 1

First Edition

Table of Contents

Introduction

We don't need scientific studies to tell us that today's culture is out of touch with nature, even though plenty of such studies exist. Not only does our world have various social pockets engaged in industrial activities that have alarming effects on the environment, but also few of us post-modern people are able to live our lives in harmony with the natural rhythms of the earth.

In fact, we tend to ignore them, whether consciously or not. We can make day seem like night and night seem like day. We can make winter feel like summer and summer feel like winter. We can travel from the tropics to the tundra in less than a day, from the mountains to the sea in an afternoon. We can find whatever fruit or vegetable we want in our local grocery store, regardless of the season.

In short, our natural environment has become a kind of add-on to our lives. We feel the pangs of weather changes and the panic of natural disasters, but our day-to-day lives, our month-to-month lives, our year-to-year lives have, in general, gotten out of synch with the natural rhythms of the earth we were created to inhabit.

This causes problems. As humans, we are *meant* to unfold our lives in harmony with the natural world. The seasons, the processes of nature, the *rhythms* of this world—our world—were created out of love and given to us as a home. They have something to tell us about our deeper identity, the purpose of our life, the way to fully live life. By cutting us off from direct, regular, and necessary contact with this natural environment, our technology-laden culture is threatening to sever an ancient and irreplaceable link to authentic wisdom. That's why I decided to write these meditations.

A Needed Return to Natural Wisdom

The bite-sized chapters in these meditation books (this is the second of four) will provide you with some space to remember and reconnect with this essential dimension of your humanity. That, by the way, is what meditation means: giving yourself the time and space, both physically and psychologically, to reflect calmly and deeply on important spiritual values. It is our sincere hope that by doing so you will experience a spiritual and emotional revitalization. You will be able to escape from the ceaseless, inhuman, digitized grind of life and regain balance.

I'm not accusing you of being unspiritual. I'm banking on the fact that even though you have hope, and courage, and faith, and love, you still feel a hunger to have *more* of them—a deeper faith, a more vibrant hope, a more dynamic courage. That's one of the great things about spiritual values. Because they are spiritual, they can always keep growing.

Avoiding the Rush

This volume only contains twelve meditations, one per week of the season. But at the end of each meditation you will find some suggested activities to help you absorb the nourishing truths the meditation explained (the *Making It Your Own* sections). A good way to make use of this book is to read a meditation at the beginning of the week underlining, highlighting, and writing in the margins as you reflect on what you read. Then for the rest of the week, take time each day to review your highlights and to put into practice one of the suggested activities. Following that method will assure that whatever good ideas you find as you read will have sufficient time and space to seep from your mind into your heart and your spirit, fostering personal renewal.

Getting Personal

These meditations contain many personal anecdotes that I think help illustrate my points. I also hope that making myself vulnerable in this way will encourage you to reflect on the richness of your own life experience to find the lessons, the nuggets of wisdom, that God, in his generous providence, always offers to you.

May this small volume of simple meditations on the season of summer be a window through which you can discover, once again, the "dearest freshness deep down things"[1] that have always nourished what is best in the human spirit.

---

[1] From Gerard Manley Hopkins' poem "God's Grandeur"

Chapter 1: *Wisdom*

Summer has two contradictory personalities. On the one hand, it's a season meant for hard work—just watch a farmer or a rancher sweating from sunup to sundown during the hot summer months. On the other hand, we tend to associate summer with relaxation; the pleasant weather lends itself to vacations and rest. It takes wisdom to know how to balance these two conflicting summer trends. The wise person will recognize both opportunities and maximize each.

This is the wisdom of summer: taking advantage of the opportunities life presents to us instead of letting them slip by unseen.

We desperately need this brand of wisdom. We face opportunities to grow and to help others grow every day, but we don't always recognize them. Even when we do recognize them, it's much easier to make excuses or put off action than it is to make these opportunities fruitful.

When a husband or wife comes home from work, he or she has within his or her grasp a golden opportunity to nourish the love that every family needs simply by giving undivided attention. How often, unfortunately, does our own exhaustion and worry blind us from seeing this chance?

When someone gifted with creativity gets a sharp new idea about how to make his parish, workplace, or community better, that also is an opportunity. It's a chance to make this world a better place while at the same time fulfilling one's own potential. Too often though, another voice takes over. That voice starts to complain about how hard it will be to make a change and all the obstacles that will have to be overcome. This voice of fear and sloth often convinces us to see golden opportunities as mere pipe dreams.

It's funny how certain regrets never really go away, even seemingly insignificant ones. I was the cocaptain of the varsity football team during my senior year of high school. The previous year we had had resounding success. We were named one of the best teams in the city and only lost one game that year. But my senior year got off to a slow start. After losing our first few games, triumph turned to discouragement and desperation in the locker room. As cocaptain, I felt I needed to do something about it. I had to show some leadership and help turn things around. But I didn't know how. Then an opportunity presented itself.

We were playing a local rival, and our offense was off to a good start in the first quarter. I was a running back, but I was also playing linebacker on defense, so I was pretty tired. I knew I wasn't a good linebacker. In fact, it was a new position for me.

As the first half unfolded, I saw a pattern emerging. We would have a few good drives on offense, but then I would get tired and we would stall. At halftime I got an idea. If the coach would take me out on defense and substitute me with our quarterback—a much better linebacker than me—I believed we had a better shot at slowing the opposition's offensive momentum. I remember I actually felt excited about this idea. My heartbeat got faster and I experienced a surge of energy. So I turned and looked for the coach to share my idea. But when I saw him, I stopped. I thought to myself that he had probably already come up with the same idea and dismissed it, that he would resent my interference, that he had too much on his mind already. So I never said a thing.

I don't know if it was as brilliant an idea as I thought, but we'll never know. We lost that game and every other game that year. Ever since, I've wondered what would have happened if I had shared that idea with the coach; if I'd done *something* with the opportunity that idea created. It certainly couldn't have hurt, and maybe it would have helped. Maybe it would have been a turning point in the season. Or maybe nothing would have changed. But at least I would have had the satisfaction of knowing I'd done my part to the full. But I didn't. I fumbled the opportunity.

Life gives us opportunities, and the wise person recognizes and takes advantage of them when they come. We don't know if they'll come back again. If a farmer puts off the work he needs to do to make his crops bear fruit, there will come a time when it's simply too late, and he will go hungry. As Proverbs 6:6–11 puts it:

> Go to the ant, O sluggard, study her ways and learn wisdom;
>
> For though she has no chief, no commander or ruler,
>
> She procures her food in the summer, stores up her provisions in the harvest.
>
> How long, O sluggard, will you lie there? When will you rise from your sleep?
>
> A little sleep, a little slumber, a little folding of the arms to rest—
>
> Then poverty will come upon you like a robber, and want like a brigand.

One of the saddest passages in the Gospels has to do with a missed opportunity. A young man who is sincerely searching for the meaning of life comes to Jesus with a question. He fights his way through the crowd and finally kneels before the Lord, asking him what he must do to obtain eternal life. The Bible tells us how the Lord opened his heart to the young man and gave him a chance to bring his life to the next level. Here's what happened:

> Jesus, looking at him, loved him and said to him, "You are lacking in one thing. Go, sell what you have, and give to [the] poor and you will have treasure in heaven; then come, follow me." At that statement his face fell, and he went away sad, for he had many possessions (Mark 10:21–22).

We have all "gone away sad" at times. We have all seen or felt opportunities, and let them pass by untapped. But we don't have to do that anymore. We can learn to be wiser, to order our lives better, so that when the many chances of summer come our way, we can welcome them all. There is a time to work hard and a time to relax, a time to do something and a time to let things be. The wise person understands the differences.

Making It Your Own

† Choose one sentence from this chapter that really resonated in your heart or compose a one-sentence summary. Write it on a sticky note. Put it where you will see it throughout the week as a reminder that wisdom involves taking advantage of opportunities.

† Take time this week to reflect prayerfully on some past opportunities you didn't take advantage of. Ask yourself why you let them pass by. Put a name on the reasons and influences that moved you to make the wrong decision (or no decision) so you will be able to recognize them if they try to disrupt you again.

† Achieving a good rhythm of work and rest in today's world isn't easy. Innumerable sources of entertainment and distraction are at our fingertips, and there's no limit to how many hours we can spend at the office. It's up to each one of us to find a healthy balance. Do you tend to be a procrastinator or a workaholic? Do you choose relaxation to the detriment of responsibility? Are you hyper-responsible and unable to relax? Write down the patterns of your life and choose to make at least one adjustment this week to improve.

† Reflect on this: What opportunities are presenting themselves to me now, in this season of my life? How am I responding to them? Choose one and make a commitment to respond to it.

† Reflect on the important people in your life. Do you feel that one is squandering an opportunity? Invite him or her out for a cup or coffee (or ice cream, or lunch) and try to give the individual encouragement, even if all that means is listening to the person's worries and concerns.

Chapter 2: *Hospitality*

Summer is filled with socializing, parties of all kinds, vacations, and visits with friends and family. The weather invites us to get out and hang out. The days are long and bright. The nights are fragrant and balmy. Summer seems to tell us what our moms told us when we were kids—*go out and play with your friends!* It is a hospitable season that moves us to cultivate interpersonal encounters and to share and enjoy the graces of generous hospitality.

Human beings are supposed to be hospitable. We are supposed to be open to others, open to receive what they have to give us and to give from our own unique personality. True hospitality is what makes human communities truly human. We have all experienced it—the sense of wonder and warmth that floods our soul when someone sincerely welcomes us into his home or shares something delicious. That same sense of wonder and satisfaction is even more intense, perhaps, when we are the ones welcoming or sharing and we detect that the other person has truly enjoyed and benefited from what we offered.

True hospitality begins with goodness of heart and overflows into all the other elements: food, drinks, decorations, music, and everything else. True hospitality welcomes another person by saying—sometimes with words, sometimes in other ways—"You really matter and I'm glad you're here." Hearing that makes our souls sing! The fruitful warmth and brightness of summer is a living parable of the fruitful warmth and brightness that flows from a genuinely hospitable heart.

The genius of femininity has historically been linked to this core value of hospitality. I believe women seem gifted in a special way with the capacity to welcome, to relate, to truly see and engage others right where they are. I was nine years old and visiting my mother for the last time when I first realized this capacity for hospitality.

My mother had multiple sclerosis and had been declining over the course of two years. At this point, she was already confined to a bed in a nursing home, and the doctors didn't give her much more time. My dad took my two sisters and me to visit her. Each of us has different memories of that visit. I didn't realize it was going to be the last time I would ever see my mom.

My memory of that visit is still vivid. It was around Christmas, and something momentous had just happened in my nine-year-old life: I had joined my first basketball league. I was on a real team, had a real uniform, and was looking forward to what I was sure would be an unforgettable championship season. Nothing else in the entire world was as important as that. So while we were driving to visit my mom, I was filled with anticipation—I couldn't wait to give her the news.

When we arrived at the nursing home, my dad took us quietly into her room. She was lying down, emaciated and exhausted, but still Mom. I remember that my dad brought each one of us to her to speak with her individually, even though she seemed barely awake and almost completely unable to talk. When my turn came, I hopped over to her bedside and told my story with great enthusiasm and gusto.

I was too small to think about what my mother was suffering. At that moment, I deeply needed her to understand my happiness. I needed her affirmation. I needed someone to say that I mattered. And that's exactly what my mother told me. I don't remember if she actually said anything in response, but I do remember what she did. She looked at me, right into the eyes, and smiled. A big smile. A smile that lit up her whole face. That smile told me everything I needed to know. It told me that she was happy that I was happy, that I mattered to her, that what was important to me was important to her, and that I, too, was important.

Over the years I have gone back to that encounter in my imagination many times, savoring it and discovering new levels of meaning. In a sense, what I experienced in my mother's smile was a profound welcome, an existentially charged gesture of true hospitality.

We are designed by our Creator to need each other, to be enriched by each other, not to be self-sufficient and isolated: "It is not good for the man to be alone…" (Genesis 2:18). Our lives are meant to be a continual exchange of giving and receiving, of encountering others and allowing them to encounter us. Only through these relationships do our true identities receive the spiritual nourishment they need to unfold and flourish. We need to give others the joy of knowing they matter by welcoming them with a sincere and interested smile. And we need to discover our own dignity and worth over and over again in the sincere smiles of others. Even the Bible links love—the very meaning of life—with the virtue of hospitality:

> Let mutual love continue. Do not neglect hospitality, for through it some have unknowingly entertained angels (Hebrews 13:1–2).

Hospitality is hard. At times we feel we simply don't have anything left to give. Our cupboards are bare, both physically and emotionally. Yet if this value is central to who we are as human beings, we shouldn't underestimate ourselves. Just because we may not *feel* like giving doesn't mean we don't have any more to give. Throughout history, more than one saint has given away her or his last loaf of bread to a beggar only to go back to the pantry and find it miraculously restocked. As St. Francis of Assisi put it, "It is in giving that we receive," and as our Lord himself said:

> Give and gifts will be given to you; a good measure, packed together, shaken down, and overflowing, will be poured into your lap. For the measure with which you measure will in return be measured out to you (Luke 6:38).

Let's take God up on his word. Let's find ways to practice this ancient, beautifully human virtue of hospitality—even when all we have to offer is a smile.

Making It Your Own

† Choose one sentence from this chapter that really resonated in your heart or compose a one-sentence summary. Write it on a sticky note. Put it where you will see it throughout the week as a reminder of the power and the goodness of hospitality.

† Take time this week to reflect prayerfully on past experiences when you have felt welcome. What were the circumstances? Why did you feel welcome? How did that feeling affect your state of mind or your decisions? Go deep with these reflections and turn this virtue into a personal value. It may help you to write out descriptions of your experiences.

† Think back to a time when you have exercised hospitality. What factors made those experiences fulfilling? What factors made them frustrating? What are your expectations when serving others? Are those the right expectations to have? Could you adjust them to become more focused on giving?

† Accept an invitation this week. Accept it with an open, generous spirit, and give yourself permission to thoroughly enjoy the hospitality that is being offered to you. Trust that, by allowing yourself to feel loved and valued by the person doing the inviting, you are increasing the amount of grace and spiritual light in the world.

† Throughout this week, think of all your interactions with people in terms of hospitality. Welcome others, whether chance encounters at the grocery store, official meetings, family meals, or whatever it may be. Welcome others with your attitude, your facial expression, and your words. Focus on being sincerely open from the first moments of the encounter. Do this all week long and keep an eye on what happens. Take time at the end the week to reflect prayerfully on what you learned. Maybe even write the lessons down.

Chapter 3: *Endurance*

Summer storms are crucial for healthy crops. It's not just because their ample downpours provide water (so does simple irrigation). It's the storm itself. Summer storms provide nourishment unavailable from any other source.

A farmer explained this to me. Good soil offers plants plenty of nourishment. Among the most important are nitrates. Water that comes into the soil from irrigation doesn't affect the nitrate concentration at all, but water that comes into the soil from a summer thunderstorm does. The clouds that produce the water pick up ions with every lightning flash. The stormy rainwater transfers these ions into the soil, where they pile up into rich deposits of nitrates. The more violent the storm, the higher the concentration of ions in the rainwater, and the richer the soil becomes. Summer storms are one of nature's creative ways to foster hardy and fruitful growth.

This natural process should give us hope. Life in this fallen world brings plenty of storms, some gentle, some violent. Through God's providence, enduring these storms can make us better. They can help us grow in wisdom, patience, fortitude, and compassion. Suffering, from God's perspective and through the influence of his grace, has a purpose, a purpose that will be achieved to the extent that we accept and endure without giving up.

One of the biggest storms I have experienced as a priest has to do with the history of my religious order. The Legionaries of Christ were founded in 1941, in Mexico, by a young Mexican priest. He was to spend the remaining sixty-seven years of his priesthood building and governing the order and the Ecclesial Movement, *Regnum Christi*, of which it is a part. After he died, a series of events led us to discover that he had been leading a double life throughout his years of ministry. He had committed deeply destructive and scandalous financial and sexual sins during the very years when our order and movement grew and expanded.

When the verified news reached us, it stirred up a devastating storm, shaking the foundations of our identity as a spiritual family in the Catholic Church. The Vatican initiated an official visitation of the entire order to detect whether the sins of the founder had corrupted the DNA of the order itself. Many members left, convinced the entire congregation was irredeemable. Many others believed the pope would dissolve the order. Instead, he decided to oversee a thorough revision and reform involving every single Legionary, a process that brought new waves of uncertainty and suffering into our communities.

This storm lasted for years. Every time it seemed to be calming down, some new development would bring back the raging winds and destructive floods. What was most painful for me was seeing so many of my companions leave the order, men I had gone through formation with, worked with, and come to admire, respect, and love. I couldn't understand why God would permit this family to break up, why such sincere and dedicated men could have such divergent convictions about what God was doing in our spiritual family.

As horrible and destructive as the situation was, its results have been positive, both for the order itself and for me personally. When my order was flourishing and crowned with success after success, I took an unhealthy pride in being a member. I often drew unfair comparisons between us and other orders in the Church, as if we were in competition to be the best religious order.

This also affected the day-to-day ministry of my priesthood. I tended to make rash judgments and lacked the serenity to truly listen to people. The storm we endured stripped away some of those self-centered attitudes and nourished essential priestly virtues like mercy, compassion, and patience. I am sure that the Lord will send future storms to keep filling up my soul with necessary "nitrates," so that those good spiritual plants can keep growing. It's already clear to me that the storm he sent during my first ten years of priesthood has made me a better priest, a better messenger of God's goodness and redemption. That storm was transformed for me by God's providence into a stimulus for spiritual growth.

Another way to understand how God's providence transforms suffering is to see it through the lens of the Gospels. In the Gospels, Jesus Christ ends up being rejected, condemned, tortured, and killed by the very people he came to forgive and save. The first Good Friday was the most tragic day in the history of the world, the day on which the human family crucified our divine Savior. It was a day of almost infinite suffering, a day of the most violent moral and spiritual storms that can be imagined.

The story didn't end with the crucifixion, though. Jesus—who is both a man and the second person of the Holy Trinity—suffered willingly, out of love. Because he refused to lash out at his enemies and instead chose to forgive them, that horrific tragedy became the very currency of salvation and the door to eternal life. On the third day after he died on the cross, Jesus rose from the dead to live forever and never die again.

The storm of Good Friday transformed the soil of this fallen world into the fertile life of Easter. Through our faith in Jesus and our reception of the sacrament of baptism, we become his brothers and sisters—children of God. We share in both Christ's cross and his resurrection. Here's how St. Paul explains it:

> The Spirit itself bears witness with our spirit that we are children of God, and if children, then heirs, heirs of God and joint heirs with Christ, if only we suffer with him so that we may also be glorified with him (Romans 8:16–17).

Suffering is unavoidable in life. Too often we forget that. Too often we believe the billboards and the commercials that try to seduce us into thinking that buying the right products will bring us heaven on earth. Not true. Suffering is part of this world. It flows from the evil and sin that entered our human story in the Garden of Eden. We can't avoid it. If we make it our goal in life to minimize suffering, we will miss the whole point of life. We will never emerge from the cocoon of self-absorption, we will never have the soil of our hearts enriched by the storm, we will never discover the depths of the beauty of true love—the love that endures and grows and stays faithful through crosses and tears.

At the end of history, when God brings forth the new heavens and the new earth, suffering will be no more: "He will wipe every tear from their eyes, and there shall be no more death or mourning, wailing or pain, [for] the old order has passed away" (Revelation 21:4). But for now, we need to let ourselves be convinced that the storms God permits in our lives have a purpose and that he will always give us the strength we need to endure them and benefit from them. We just need to keep on believing, hoping, and loving, as hard as doing so may get. And we can, if we keep Christ's cross in sight. By persevering through his crucifixion, Jesus opened the path to the resurrection, a path we are all called to follow:

> Consider it all joy, my brothers, when you encounter various trials, for you know that the testing of your faith produces perseverance. And let perseverance be perfect, so that you may be perfect and complete, lacking in nothing (James 1:2–4).

The next time you witness a summer storm, think about that, and thank God for giving you chances to enrich the soil of your soul and produce bumper crops of spiritual goods.

Making It Your Own

† Choose one sentence from this chapter that really resonated in your heart or compose a one-sentence summary. Write it on a sticky note. Put it where you will see it throughout the week as a reminder that summer storms have a nourishing purpose.

† What has been the most recent storm in your life? Reflect prayerfully on it; open yourself to the grace God wants to send you through it. If it helps, write a letter to the Lord expressing your feelings.

† Take time this week to read slowly and prayerfully Psalms 22 and 23. Psalm 22 expresses the agony of immense suffering through vivid and poetic imagery. It was the psalm Jesus himself invoked as he was dying on the cross. But even though it begins with suffering and deep pain, it ends with hope. Psalm 23, the Good Shepherd psalm, takes up the theme of hope. Together, these psalms put into inspired words our own contradictory experiences of feeling abandoned but simultaneously loved by God. They should be familiar prayers for all of us.

† Think about the people you know. Who is going through a stormy time? This week, reach out to that person and offer some encouragement. Remind him or her that storms have a purpose and will come to an end eventually.

† Take time this week to think back on the biggest storms you have had to go through in your life. Write down the lessons they taught you and the benefits they brought you. If you can't identify the lessons and benefits, reach out to a friend or mentor and talk about the storm. Ask this trusted person to help you discover and accept how God's hand was at work through that experience.

Chapter 4: *Kindness*

Summer is a gentle season. It is kind. The lush green grass invites you to lie down and relax, to stay on your back and watch the blue sky and powdery clouds dance lazily on by. They even say that gazing on the color green, the dominant color of the summer months, produces relaxing physiological effects. The warm sun caresses your skin and makes you smile. The balmy breezes give you hugs that make you want to run and jump and play. Even some of the thorn bushes become friendly, offering wild berries to delight your palate and nourish your body. Summer is kind and bountiful.

Kindness may not be the most profound or theological value in the human family, but it sure comes close. Think about it. What would life be like if all kindness were dissolved from human interaction? It's unimaginable. It would no longer be human. To be treated with respect and affection meets our fundamental need to be affirmed and to engage in relationships with other people. We know that it's a basic need because when we experience it, we echo it. Kindness is contagious. When people treat us kindly, we tend to be more likely to treat others kindly, and the whole network of human interactions is enhanced with goodness, beauty, and greater happiness. Take kindness away and the world becomes nothing more than a prison, a colony of human mechanisms or, even worse, of human beasts. Kindness matters, and we should never take it for granted.

One of my most transformative experiences of kindness happened during my junior year of college, when I was taking a semester abroad in Florence, Italy. We had a few weeks off for Christmas vacation and my host family helped arrange for me to spend some of that time living in the mystical, medieval city of Assisi, a place I came to love dearly. My first stop was at a palazzo built right into the city wall, a palazzo that was the home of an elderly woman named Maria Boenni.

Maria lived alone, and the plan was for me to spend a few days boarding with her. She would provide a place to sleep and I would explore the artistic, architectural, historical, and spiritual treasures of St. Francis' native town.

I knocked on her door not knowing what to expect. She opened the door, and I was face to face with a petite elderly woman who exuded elegance, simplicity, and an absolutely radiant kindness.

She escorted me in and showed me around. Her home had taken on her personality. Every piece of furniture and décor, it seemed, was smiling at me, welcoming me with open arms. Besides being exquisite, it was also warm—like a summer breeze or a meadow in summer sunshine.

She showed me to her patio, which offered a breathtaking view of the Umbrian valley, and eventually brought me to my room. She instructed me to settle in, freshen up, and, whenever I was ready, join her in the parlor for tea.

When I was ready, I went to have tea. I had never had tea before. I sat in a chair that felt like a throne, and Maria made her way in and out of the kitchen, chatting enjoyably and making me feel very important. She brought out the tray and asked, "Do you take milk or lemon in your tea?" I froze. What was the proper response? What were you supposed to do? What was the polite option, the correct option, the cultured option? I had no idea. "Well, um, both, thank you," I finally spluttered out. She barely suppressed a chuckle, but her smile was as warm as the tea. Later I discovered that you aren't supposed to mix lemon and milk in your tea. It's not only a *faux pas*; it's also unhealthy. But Maria didn't give me a single disapproving vibe in response.

That set the tone for three unequivocally delightful days. We would eat breakfast together in the morning, have tea in the afternoon, and in between I explored Assisi. Every day she would get me talking about my adventures, and she would share her insights and suggestions. She treated me with gentleness and respect, like an equal, though I felt far from that. She bathed me in kindness, and without realizing it my soul began to flourish.

In that short visit, Maria changed me. Her wise and genuine kindness opened my mind and heart to a different way of being. I couldn't have put words to it then, but I definitely felt it.

Kindness matters. We shouldn't take it for granted. In the Bible, kindness is consistently praised and linked to the deepest value of all: love.

Saint Paul puts kindness near the top of the list of expressions of love: "Love is patient, love is kind," he writes. He also includes it with the fruits of the Holy Spirit, "In contrast, the fruit of the Spirit is love, joy, peace, patience, kindness, generosity, faithfulness, gentleness, self-control." At one point, he sums up Christian behavior by saying: "Your kindness should be known to all." Jesus himself encourages us to cultivate kindness by following his own example: "Take my yoke upon you and learn from me, for I am meek and humble of heart; and you will find rest for yourselves" (1 Corinthians 13:4, Galatians 5:22–23, Philippians 4:5, Matthew 11:29).

Kindness isn't everything, but it's close. True kindness refuses to harm others and habitually treats others with respect, dignity, and goodness. It flows from the conviction that every person is as infinitely valuable as oneself, and so it is a primary way to fulfill the Golden Rule.

Sometimes kindness has to overflow into chivalry, into efforts to protect others from harm. This is why authentic kindness doesn't tolerate or condone sinful behavior or decisions. If someone I know wants to rob a bank, only *false* kindness will agree to give that person a ride to the scene of the crime. *True* kindness will try to talk some sense into the errant acquaintance. Kindness may seem like weakness to some, but in fact it is the fruit of great spiritual strength.

When we make kindness a personal value and goal, we bring summer's warmth and brightness to people's souls. And in a world that seems to be leaning further and further toward a spiritual winter, that's no small contribution.

Making It Your Own

† Choose one sentence from this chapter that really resonated in your heart or compose a one-sentence summary. Write it on a sticky note. Put it where you will see it throughout the week as a reminder that kindness matters and shouldn't be taken for granted.

† Take one day this week and keep track of every act of kindness that comes your way. Jot them down after they happen. At the end of the day, read over the list and ask yourself how each of those acts of kindness made you feel.

† Take one day this week in which you will make kindness your top priority. On that day, in every encounter and task, intentionally behave with absolute kindness. At the end of the day, take time to prayerfully reflect on how you felt and how your kindness affected the events of the day.

† Who in your life do you tend to be unkind with? Often we fall into unkindness with the people closest to us, those we should treat with even greater respect and dignity. After you have identified the person you tend to be unkind toward, think about how you can make it up to that person. Think about something

you can do to show a commitment to treat the individual with true kindness from now on. Write that commitment on your calendar so you remember to follow through with it.

† What is the kindest thing that has been done to you in the last month (or the last week)? Think about it. Let yourself feel grateful for it, and then make a commitment to return that act of kindness with another act of kindness, either to the kind person or to someone else as a way to spread the warmth of summer. Decide what that act will be and put it on your calendar so you remember it.

Chapter 5: *Modesty*

Summer's heat invites relaxation. Often it's just too hot to exert oneself. It also invites a certain casual air—being formal in the summertime is uncomfortable, so we loosen our standards, whether in behavior, speech, or dress. A little more joking, a little more flirtation, a little longer happy hour, and a little less clothing are all simply par for the course during the hot summer months.

In theory, there's nothing wrong with that. Actually, it would be strange if we behaved the same during the winter months as during the summer months. We are not robots and we are not angels. Our physical, geographical, and climatic environments affect our attitudes and actions. They are beautiful parts of being human.

However, it's possible to go too far. After all, even though we aren't angels, we aren't beasts, either. It's possible to fall into too much joking, flirtation, and drinking; it's possible to wear too little clothing; it's possible to loosen our standards excessively and break down the atmosphere of respect and dignity we need in order to make truly wise decisions. Modesty, as unpopular and scarce as it may be, is the virtue that helps us find the right balance.

We usually associate modesty with clothes. That's a good place to begin, but it doesn't stop there. Modesty is a value, a form of prudence that enables us to discern not only how much skin it is wise to reveal on a particular occasion but also how much of what we are feeling or thinking should be revealed in this or that situation. Modesty involves the capacity for elegant and reasonable self-restraint, exercised in harmony with the needs and expectations, as well as the opportunities and dangers, of each unique social context. Immodesty always involves a certain inappropriateness that harms and wounds others, as well as ourselves.

I used to think that modesty was something only women had to worry about. They shouldn't dress provocatively, because when they do they make it hard for men to avoid falling into lustful thoughts. That is a valid expression of modesty. Dressing provocatively or even carelessly can create occasions of sin and end up contradicting our own desire to be treated like persons instead of like mere objects of pleasure.

But modesty isn't just about avoiding provocative dress and it isn't just for women.

Modesty has a positive, more universal function as well. Finding the right balance in our behavior and dress can help create environments for fruitful human interactions. We have to understand the social context and adjust to it reasonably and wisely.

I had an enlightening experience in this regard after I had been a priest for several years. As a member of a religious order, I had been trained to maintain a certain formality in my dress and interaction. This is an expression of respect for the people I interact with, as well as a way of avoiding worldly habits that could interfere with my spiritual commitments. But I was to discover that excessive formality (a less well-known form of immodesty) could actually inhibit living out those values.

I was in California for some meetings and work sessions about launching a new apostolate (a website now called RCSpirituality.org). The core team was coming together for the first time. We spent a day meeting with an expert business consultant to get some feedback on our approach and our strategy. The next day, the core team was going to meet to digest what we had learned from the previous session without any outside consultants.

We were meeting close to one of the residences of my religious order, so I showed up dressed in my regular religious habit. For me, that was the most normal thing to wear. But the other members of the team, who were laypeople in different states of life, had come dressed more casually. The formal meeting, they understood, had taken place the day before; today was a let's-get-to-work-and-roll-up-our-sleeves type meeting. When I showed up in my cassock, they all balked. They felt out of place, uncomfortable, and unable to dive into the task at hand. I sensed the discomfort quickly but wasn't sure where it was coming from. Eventually I asked, and they told me. From what they said, it was as if I had shown up to a backyard barbecue sporting a tuxedo. Awkward, especially for them. I changed into something more appropriate.

Just as we pay careful attention to what is appropriate in the decoration of our places of worship, we are also called to pay attention to how we present ourselves. As St. Paul reminds us, every Christian is like a living place of worship because the Blessed Trinity dwells within us:

> Do you not know that your body is a temple of the holy Spirit within you, whom you have from God, and that you are not your own? For you have been purchased at a price. Therefore glorify God in your body (1 Corinthians 6:19–20).

A well-known story from the life of St. Jane Frances de Chantal illustrates some of these practical implications. Jane was the daughter of a French nobleman and married the baron of Chantal when she was twenty years old. They had a grace-filled marriage blessed with the gift of six children (three of whom died very young). Deeply in love, their estate was the envy of all their peers, not only in prosperity, but especially in familial happiness. This robust marital joy was no accident. Mr. and Mrs. Chantal knew how to guard their hearts from vain and destructive fancies. Once a friend commented on how modestly Jane dressed whenever her husband was away. Her reply was full of Christian wisdom, "The eyes which I want to please are a hundred miles from here."

Their joyful marriage lasted only nine years, ending when the baron was killed in a hunting accident. Jane's grief hurtled her into acute depression. She refused to consider remarrying and instead began increasing her religious devotion. Jane asked God to send her someone who could be her guide along the way to deeper intimacy with Christ. Her prayers were answered, and she soon crossed paths with St. Francis de Sales.

Jane de Chantal, alongside her friend and spiritual director, St. Francis de Sales, became the foundress of the Order of the Visitation of Holy Mary. By her death at age 69, she had established sixty-five convents.

Our dress, speech, and behavior communicate something to those around us. We do not live in isolation from our neighbors, and it is self-centered to think that we should be free to do whatever we feel like, regardless of how it will affect others. On the other hand, the deeper reasons behind our choices in these matters should be based on principles, not just what other people may think. Modesty is the applied wisdom that helps us find a fruitful equilibrium.

Those principles that should dictate our choices are beautiful and powerful. We are created in God's image and likeness. We have been redeemed by Jesus' sacrificial love. We are invited by Jesus to become, through faith and baptism, a child of God and to grow into a saint. We are called to be spiritually mature, unique personalities that reflect the glory of God.

Christ is a king, the eternal king, the only king whose kingdom will last forever. As his followers we have been made sharers in his divine nobility. We can delight in showing that nobility not only through our moral integrity and spiritual creativity but also through dressing and behaving with appropriate, elegant, and charming simplicity. Modesty helps us bring beauty and harmony back into a world gone mad. It's not a bad word at all. On the contrary, it helps summer joys stay joyful.

Making It Your Own

† Choose one sentence from this chapter that really resonated in your heart or compose a one-sentence summary. Write it on a sticky note. Put it where you will see it throughout the week as a reminder that modesty is a joy-giving form of practical wisdom.

† Take time this week to examine the motivations behind how you choose to dress. Where do they come from? How can you adjust them in light of modesty?

† Our culture has a tradition of dressing up to go to church. How would you explain to someone the reasons behind this tradition? How convinced are you of the value of this tradition? What criteria do you think should govern what we wear to church, and why?

† During the Golden Age of Hollywood, movie producers agreed to a certain level of modesty in their films. It was called the Hays Code and contained guidelines and specific prohibitions to help movies avoid having a corrosive effect on morality. In the late 1960s, it was replaced by the current Motion Picture Association of America film-rating system (G, PG, and so on). What effect, if any, do you think what we

watch and listen to can have on our sense of modesty? How carefully do you choose what you watch and listen to? How carefully would you/do you choose what your children watch and listen to? Is there a difference in the level of care? If so, why?

† This week, take a few hours with a friend and visit an art museum. Don't try to see everything, but visit rooms that display art from different periods and different cultures. Reflect together on the messages being portrayed by the different works of art and how those messages are communicated. What feelings do the different works stir up in you? What aspirations or desires do they stimulate? Use this visit to regain sensitivity to the communicative power of our external gestures (clothing, posture, facial expressions, and more).

Chapter 6: *Playfulness*

Most people go on some kind of vacation during the summer months. We need vacations. We need time to rest, to relax, to recover from the demanding physical, mental, and psychological exertions required in this world.

But have you ever ended your vacation feeling even more exhausted than you felt at the beginning? Have you ever arrived to Monday morning—after a weekend that is supposed to be restful—more exhausted than you were on Friday afternoon? You probably have. Most people have. This is because, at least in part, our culture has forgotten the art of playfulness. We no longer remember what healthy relaxation looks like.

Various studies have explored this phenomenon in different contexts. The basic conundrum seems to be that people are more stressed out now than ever before. The increase of tension and anxiety that goes along with this creates physiological health problems (high cholesterol, sleep disorders, chronic fatigue) as well as psychosocial health problems (breakdown of family unity, childhood and adult depression, substance abuse). An inability to find and maintain the proper balance between hard work and healthy relaxation has become a kind of epidemic in our culture. More and more, we tend to be obsessive and extreme both at work and at play, crippling the true interior harmony that allows our souls to grow and flourish. There aren't any quick fixes for this problem. But we also can't ignore it.

Here again we can learn so much from the rhythms of nature. Think about the long, gentle sunrises and sunsets that mark the summer months. There is no rush to them. Daytime dawns gradually and organically, then fades away with equal elegance. The wisdom of nature is constantly inviting us to greater harmony and balance, if only we could truly slow down enough to hear it.

The two best vacations I ever had were right before I started high school and right before I started college. In both cases, because of the academic transition I was going through, I didn't really have any school or sports responsibilities carrying over through the summer, which gave me a sense of freedom. But more than that, what made these vacations so wonderful was the sheer, profound playfulness that characterized them.

While I was growing up, my dad took an annual vacation to Ontario, Canada. He and an old friend would go on fishing trips, canoeing through a wilderness lake region where both of them had gone to camp as kids. They would drive through the night to get there, park the car, throw the canoe in the water, and leave civilization behind for ten or fifteen days.

I always wanted to join my dad on these trips. He would be so excited to go, and when he came back he would be so relaxed and happy. I just knew that something special happened in Canada. But I was always too small and too young. Then, after finishing eighth grade, my dad informed me that I finally qualified. And so I joined the adventure.

As we took the long drive north, I could feel the tension begin to drain from my dad. By the time we got to our first campsite, it was almost as if he were a different person. He had a tough life raising three kids by himself and was usually anxious and stressed. But in Canada, a thousand miles from home and weighty cares and responsibilities, he changed. He smiled almost all the time. He laughed and joked. He listened. He taught me how to chop wood, bait a hook, cast a lure—and he didn't get mad when I messed up.

The rest of us would sleep in tents, but my dad would sleep on the open ground or on a dock, even when it was chilly. He said he liked to go to sleep looking at the stars.

At times during our trip I would catch him

just standing on the shore of a lake, gazing at the beauty of the virgin forests. Sitting around the campfire, he and his old friend would reminisce and cut each other down good-humoredly, including me in the conversation.

Those were the best vacations I remember, because they truly were *vacations*. Our English word comes from the Latin word *vacare*, which means "to be unoccupied." My dad would leave behind all his worries and throw himself into nature. He didn't do it all by himself, he shared it with a friend, and with his son, and with his son's friend. On those trips I discovered that my dad really knew how to play, and that taking a couple weeks a year to do that profoundly refreshed him and refilled his mental and psychological gas tank. By experiencing that with him, I was given a reference point for the rest of my life about what healthy relaxation really feels like.

Looking back on those experiences now, I am filled with gratitude but also with some regret. On vacation I got to know my dad in a different way; I discovered the depths of the person he was. But that wonderful person only made occasional appearances. Most of the time, he was bound by anxiety and tension that more often than not overflowed even into weekends and holidays. How I wish that we had been able to live a better work-rest balance in the normal rhythms of life, not just on vacation! I wish that the smiles I saw on my dad's face when we would sit around the campfire would have appeared more often when he was wearing his suit and tie.

To my mind, here lies the wisdom behind the Third Commandment, one that—according to the Judeo-Christian tradition—corresponds to the very laws of nature, the existential needs of our human nature:

> Remember the sabbath day—keep it holy. Six days you may labor and do all your work, but the seventh day is a sabbath of the LORD your God. You shall not do any work (Exodus 20:8–10).

We usually remember that the Lord's day requires us to worship, but how often do we remember that the Lord himself has also reminded us to rest from our labors, to set our work aside on a regular basis?

Worship and rest share a profound connection. Squirrels and ants never take a day off, and they never worship. They were not created in God's image, and they don't have spiritual souls. When we fail to place our work aside, we don't become more human but less. We become more like beasts or like machines. The human soul is made for more than labor. We work in order to live; we don't live in order to work (though human work does have an intrinsic value and dignity). The joys of interpersonal communion, the spiritual joys of appreciating beauty and simply feeling and glorying in the pleasure of being alive, of being loved, of loving in return—this is the heart of worship and the secret to playfulness. If we can't do that, it is likely that our work has become our god, and when that happens, we will end up worshiping nothing but ourselves.

Let's buck the trend of our culture. Let's abandon obsessive work and obsessive pleasure. Let's relearn the art of living. This summer, let's take a true vacation.

Making It Your Own

† Choose one sentence from this chapter that really resonated in your heart or compose a one-sentence summary. Write it on a sticky note. Put it where you will see it throughout the week as a reminder that playfulness is not a luxury but an essential part of living.

† Take time this week to reflect prayerfully on your past experiences of vacation. What are the good ones and what are the bad ones? Why? What can you learn from them? Get together this week with whoever will be accompanying you on this year's vacation. Start planning. Talk about what will help both (all) of you have a true and fruitful vacation.

† Take someone you trust and who knows you well out to coffee this week. Ask her or him to tell you how she or he thinks you are living your work-rest balance. Really listen. Ask for ideas about how you could improve this aspect of your life. Make a concrete commitment and ask if this person will help keep you accountable.

† What helps you relax in a healthy way? What helps you relax in an unhealthy way? How can you tell the difference? What can you do

this week to eliminate the unhealthy and take better advantage of the healthy?

† How do you deal with anxiety and stress? How could you deal with them better? What are the most common sources of anxiety in your life? What can you do to shrink or eliminate them? If you can't eliminate them, what will you do this week to respond to them in a healthy way?

Chapter 7: *Remembrance*

Summer is an active season. We do things. We fill our time with events, whether long days of hard work or long days of fun and games. Summer days are the longest of the year and summer nights are the warmest. Summer is a season when we make memories.

It's no mere coincidence that summer fosters activity and creativity. Look at the world of nature during summertime. Everything is growing and branching out. We have to cut the grass every week and keep an eye out for the daily incursion of weeds. Birds build their nests and work hard to find enough food to feed their chicks. Rabbits are busy invading our vegetable gardens, bees are busy harvesting their nectar, insects swarm, deer graze, and beavers build their dams from dawn to dusk. Summer brings a unique vitality to the natural environment.

As human beings, that natural environment is ours, too. We are as natural to it as the bees and the beavers. And so it only makes sense that our summers would also be particularly active seasons, that we would feel spurred on to work, to build (projects or relationships), to travel, explore, and discover new things. This branching out of our human spirit is what leads to fresh experiences and achievements, the stuff of which memories are made.

Unfortunately, we seem to be forgetting what to do with all those memories. Our culture is forming a new, unhealthy obsession with the latest stimulus. We are increasing the flow of new experiences at an accelerated rate and have constant access to more. We have no time to thoroughly process each experience. We miss discovering, valuing, and enjoying the treasure it has given us. Once we post a photo of where we are, we forget about the moment and look ahead anxiously to a new posting opportunity. When no such opportunity presents itself, we pull out our smartphone and scroll through everybody else's posts and messages and photos. When we're constantly looking for a distraction, we miss opportunities for reflection, contemplation, and interior silence.

Yet our human nature is still intact. And part of that nature yearns for meaning. It isn't enough to experience things. We need to discover purpose in them. We need to integrate experience into our identity. We need to know that we are coming from somewhere and going somewhere. The deeper needs of the human heart cannot be ignored for long. Living a superficial life will eventually lead us to frustration and sadness instead of fulfillment. Frustration and sadness can be powerful motivators—they can move us to turn off the TV, go offline, and turn our gaze inward for some healthy self-reflection. Creating meaningful memories requires punctuating our activities with that kind of quiet introspection; otherwise life becomes an endless run-on sentence.

To a large extent, we are who we have become through our past experiences. Those experiences—and the choices we have made in reaction to them—have shaped our personality. By taking time to reflect intentionally on our recent and distant past, we can become wiser, stronger, and happier human beings.

When I was eighteen, I believed California was the pinnacle of civilization. I loved history and felt that California was the purest and most complete example of the American ethos. So I went to California for college. Where else would I go?

I still believe in America's greatness, though my current belief is more nuanced and mature. Part of what led to that nuancing was my experience of other countries, other cultures, and a much-expanded perspective on history and historical memory. Through my university studies, and in a special way through my studies abroad, I came to understand that America didn't spring like Adam from the dust of the earth. It was, and is, part of a much larger story, a history that is worth remembering.

One of my semesters abroad was spent with a small group of American students in Kraków, Poland. This was spring 1989, so the Soviet Union was still ruling Poland as well as her eastern- and central-European neighbors. Living and studying there, especially under those circumstances, broadened my horizons immeasurably.

Exploring Kraków for me, Cleveland-born and California-educated, was like walking into a fairy tale. Kraków boasts the largest town square in Europe, one surrounded by medieval churches and other structures such as castles and walls that trace their origins back through Poland's rich millennial history. I was dazed and loving it.

My professor and I went to a large café hoping to get coffee and a snack before continuing our exploration. It was so crowded we couldn't find a single open table. Finally my professor spotted a table for four occupied by an elderly woman. He asked her if we might share the table, and she graciously consented.

The woman asked where we were from and what we were doing in Kraków. The professor answered, translating the conversation into English for me as they talked back and forth.

A few minutes into their exchange, the woman put her left arm on the table and began rolling up her sleeve. As she revealed the inside of her forearm, we saw a long number there, tattooed in black. While she showed it, she was telling us that she was Jewish and had been sent to a concentration camp after the Nazis invaded and occupied Poland in 1939. I gaped. I stared. I thought, *is this for real?*

She was the first person I met in Poland, and that brief encounter threw me into a psychological and spiritual whirlwind. Here, history wasn't something you read about in books. Here, history walked the streets and conversed with you. Here, somehow the stories from the past were more than just stories. They were realities that reached into the present and gave it shape, meaning, and depth. Here, studying history meant discovering who we are and where we have come from.

The experience in Kraków was a turning point in my life. To contemplate our past, to remember and mull over the experiences that have made us what we are—this is an art we cannot afford to lose as individuals or as a culture.

The importance of remembrance, of intentionally calling to mind the experiences of our past in a calm and reflective way, is a constant theme in the Bible. In fact, one of the most frequent complaints of the Lord against his

Chosen People is that they forget so quickly all the blessings that he has showered upon them. Their slipping into idolatry, ingratitude, injustice, and corruption was often due to a culpable forgetfulness. As the psalmist puts it: "They forgot the God who had saved them, who had done great deeds in Egypt" (Psalm 106:21).

God wants us to exercise our memories because he knows that our lives are stories of grace and mercy, stories with spiritual meaning. Only when we learn to remember the past and detect within it the guiding hand of God will we learn to trust him more. And only by trusting him will we be able to continue forward along the path of spiritual progress where he lovingly yearns to lead us, "Find your delight in the LORD, who will give you your heart's desire. Commit your way to the LORD; trust in him and he will act" (Psalm 37:4–5).

This can be hard. Not all our memories are pleasant. It can be difficult to exercise faith and find the presence of God in our lives. It requires effort to read the story of providence behind our experiences; it requires what the ancient writers used to call "asceticism." We have to train ourselves to go deep, to reflect, to pray, to wake ourselves from the comfort of forgetful superficiality, to truly *remember*.

This summer, make new memories but also nourish your mind and heart on the good memories you have already made. Don't settle for living on the surface. Go deep. Reflect on things, contemplate matters, and grow steadily in the joyful wisdom that only comes to those who, like the Blessed Virgin Mary, are truly *mindful* (that's what the Latin root of "remember" means) of everything that happens to them: "And Mary kept all these things, reflecting on them in her heart" (Luke 2:19).

Making It Your Own

† Choose one sentence from this chapter that really resonated in your heart or compose a one-sentence summary. Write it on a sticky note. Put it where you will see it throughout the week as a reminder of the power of remembrance.

† Take time this week to through old family photographs or read through old journals, letters, or diaries. Give them a chance to speak to you, and prayerfully listen to what they have to say. Ask God to help you welcome any lessons he wants to teach you.

† With a friend or with your family, take one day this week and go entirely offline. No Internet, no apps, no messaging of any sort. Live the day undigitally, focusing on healthy relaxation and face-to-face, unrushed human interaction. At the end of the day, reflect on what happened. How hard was it to do? What difference did it make in the rhythm of the day, in how you felt, in how time passed? What did you learn? Would it be worth doing on a regular basis?

† Take a trip down memory lane this week. Go to a place that was important to you at some point in your past (the house where you grew up, the school you attended as a child, the church where you received first Communion). Listen to the memories it stirs up. What are they telling you? Are you grateful for them, resentful of them? Write down what you feel as you remember.

† This week, take a friend and visit a civic or religious memorial. Take plenty of time to read the inscriptions and explanations, to contemplate the statuary, architecture, and other symbolic decorations. After the visit, pause for a cup of coffee with your friend and talk through the experience. What did you learn? How does the event commemorated by that memorial form part of your own story (personally and culturally)? What did you take away from this visit?

Chapter 8: *Celebration*

Every season has its celebrations, but summer almost always begins with one. The academic year draws to a close and someone we know is graduating, from eighth grade, high school, or college. Summer vacation starts after that commencement ceremony ends. The beginning of summer is habitually marked by celebrating real achievements. It's a special time of celebration.

This is also reflected in the many local customs associated with summer celebrations. Almost every culture has some kind of summer festival with roots in history. From the Vestalia of ancient Rome, to the summer solstice sun dance of the Sioux Native Americans, to the dozens of international music festivals held every year throughout the world. Summertime inspires a celebratory mood with its brightness and vitality. Often the celebrations are linked to the work achieved in summer. From rodeos to state fairs, good food and good fun form a happy partnership. It's easier to gather large groups of people to enjoy performances and concerts in the open air. The ancient Vikings even took advantage of the summer solstice for their annual political gatherings.

Summer has a long tradition of being a season marked by particularly boisterous traditions of celebrating. But this is more than just convenience. There is some real wisdom behind authentic celebrations.

Business consultants often have to remind their clients to take time to celebrate their achievements and their progress, even when that progress or those achievements feel small. Our culture can be ultracompetitive, and healthy celebration often takes a back seat to ambition. Instead of pausing to enjoy the good things we've done or the progress we've made, we become our own internal critic, constantly bringing up everything we still have to do. Without developing a proper capacity to celebrate, we are in danger of racing madly forward without knowing where we're supposed to be going.

Celebrations are human things. Only human beings can pause and rejoice in the good things of life. Animals don't have the capacity to detect the rhythms of work and achievement. As individuals, as families, and as communities, celebrations are material expressions of spiritual value. A birthday party, a baptism, a wedding anniversary, a graduation, a sports banquet aren't just for kids.

They're for all of us. We all need to stop and enjoy the difference we make in the world and the good gifts that come to us through God's providence.

As a priest, I have the privilege of living the rhythms of the liturgical year with great awareness. The Catholic Church celebrates the many mysteries of Jesus' life and death through an annual calendar of worshipful events, each with its own prayers, colors, traditions, and associations. It's something I value and enjoy, but I have to admit that sometimes it feels inconvenient to give these celebrations the proper space, time, and attention. Whenever I start to feel them as a burden instead of as a gift, I remember Padre Salvatore Butler and the unforgettable lesson he taught me about celebration.

Padre Salvatore was a Franciscan priest from Pittsburgh, ordained before World War II. I met him when I was in college and he was retired in the Franciscan community of San Damiano, in Assisi, Italy. He was a friend of my art history professor, who had arranged for me to stay with him and his fellow Franciscans during my Christmas vacation. At the time I was not yet Catholic, but I was beginning to fall in love with the Church. I was eager to live with the Franciscan friars and learn more about this mysterious, mystical faith that inspired so much beauty in the world.

Padre Salvatore was a generous host. I sat next to him at every meal, and he engaged me in lively conversations. After breakfast, I would go upstairs to his cell and sit with him all morning, asking questions about the Catholic Church. I was eager to learn, and he was glad to share his abundant knowledge and wisdom.

Halfway through the week, I began to get worried. Everything I was learning about the Catholic Church was making Catholicism very attractive to me, but I'd never really thought about becoming Catholic. That would be a radical step, but I began to feel that it might be the only logical step to take. It worried me so much that I couldn't sleep. So I got up around midnight and wandered over to the little chapel near my room. I went in and started to read a book of meditations that Padre Salvatore had given to me. I found myself on my knees in front of the sanctuary lamp next to the tabernacle. I poured out my heart to God in prayer. I don't know how long I stayed there, but I know that gradually the turbulence I felt in my soul subsided as a deep, supernatural peace filled my heart.

The next morning I couldn't wait to tell Padre Salvatore about it and ask him what it all meant. When I finished, breathless, I looked eagerly into his face and said, "Well, what do you think?" He shook his head, looked at me with a smile and said, "Well, this is cause for celebration." Then he leaned over, opened up a cupboard underneath his bookshelf, and pulled out a bottle of Jack Daniel's whiskey. He poured two shots and we joyously toasted my first mystical experience.

My visit to the chapel that night was a milestone on the path to discovering my priestly vocation. I don't know if Padre Salvatore understood that, but he recognized that something wonderful had happened to me that night. He affirmed it and affirmed me by offering that toast.

In the Old Testament, God had to command his Chosen People to take time to celebrate the milestones in their relationship with him. The big holidays were not just one-day affairs; they lasted for an entire week.

Every autumn they celebrated the feast of Tabernacles, during which pilgrims would come to Jerusalem and live in tents outside the city, commemorating the Exodus, the forty years when they were traveling through the wilderness on the way to the Promised Land. Every spring they celebrated the Passover, commemorating the miraculous liberation from slavery in Egypt that God worked for them through the ten plagues and the parting of the Red Sea. And fifty days later, they would celebrate Pentecost, commemorating the gift of the Law on Mount Sinai and using the occasion to offer the first fruits of their harvest to the Lord. A later winter festival was introduced in commemoration of the restoration of the Temple in Jerusalem after the Maccabean revolt against Hellenistic oppression—this celebration was called Hanukkah.

The symbols of these celebrations—light, water, unleavened bread, for example—foreshadowed many of the symbolic meanings in our own sacramental celebrations, which are the definitive fulfillment in Christ of those Old Testament events that prefigured him. These celebrations are given to us by God in order to help us live life at a deeper level, the level of everlasting purpose and eternal love.

I wonder if we toast enough. I wonder if we need to brush up on our capacity to celebrate. Not just "to party" but really *to celebrate:* to perceive the meaning of key events and achievements, to take time out to enjoy them, to name that meaning and truly value it. When we celebrate, we come together with others who also see meaning behind an event. We affirm each other and share in each other's joy.

Making It Your Own

† Choose one sentence from this chapter that really resonated in your heart or compose a one-sentence summary. Write it on a sticky note. Put it where you will see it throughout the week as a reminder to spiritualize your achievements through celebration.

† Take time this week to reflect on how you celebrate the meaningful days and achievements of your personal and family life. Write down the celebrations that are part of your life, and describe what they mean to you. What can you do to help celebrate more meaningfully?

† Meaningful celebrations are usually linked with traditions. What family traditions do you value? What personal and family rituals have you developed over the years? What can you do to weave this ancient wisdom (traditions and rituals) into your personal and family life more fruitfully?

† The next time you are gathered with friends or family for a meal and fellowship, make a point of toasting some small achievement of someone there. Enjoy the moment, the person, the achievement, and its meaning by making a spontaneous, joyful toast. Make it a habit.

† Think about an upcoming celebration in your community or your parish. How could you and your loved ones participate in it more actively or meaningfully than you have in the past. Share your commitment with someone who can help hold you accountable.

Chapter 9: *Excellence*

Even though many of us are able to take a vacation during this season, summertime still tends to be busy and full of things to do. Road crews work long hours making repairs. Contractors and landscape engineers augment their work forces to take on bigger jobs. And, of course, farmers rarely have an idle moment. Even kids on summer break fill up their days with sports and clinics and camps, where they strive to learn new skills or hone the old ones. Summer is a season of building, growing, and achieving, a season in which we set high goals and work hard to achieve them.

Something in the human spirit drives us to improve, to seek excellence in whatever we put our hands to. Our fallen nature can resist or distort this interior drive. Such resistance is most commonly known as laziness, though sometimes it shows up disguised as envy, anger, or even despair. But we all recognize and admire excellence and improvement whenever we see it. The human soul is created to make a difference in this world, to become a co-creator of the universe that God put under our care. Discovering, learning, building, and excelling flow naturally from our fundamental human vocation to "fill the earth and subdue it" (Genesis 1:28). We derive satisfaction from doing a good job, and that's a healthy satisfaction linked to the very purpose of our lives.

Growing up, I always played sports in the summer. As soon as I was old enough, I joined local little-league baseball teams, just like all my buddies. Usually I could walk or ride my bike to practices and games, and I loved getting there early. I loved the competition and the challenge. I wanted to be great. At first, I understood greatness in terms of my own personal performance: hitting more home runs than anyone else, pitching more strikeouts, making more spectacular plays. But my point of view changed the summer my dad volunteered to coach.

My dad had been an elite athlete. He was also recruited right out of high school to play professional baseball. He spent seven years in the minor leagues constantly battling injuries. He never stopped loving athletics though. When he decided to coach our little-league team, he didn't just go through the motions. He poured himself into it. I was only about twelve years old, but I made a point of hanging out nearby whenever he was on the phone to listen to him analyze and plan how to help my team excel.

At our first practice, he started giving kids hitting instructions. Very quickly he realized that most of the kids had never really had authentic coaching. The dads who usually coached had never played professionally. They barely knew the fundamentals and didn't know how to help the kids grow and develop. My dad changed the system. He split the team into two groups and had each group practice separately. This enabled each kid to get twice as much time in the field and more personalized attention. It also meant that my dad had to dedicate twice as much time to coaching. He didn't think anything of it. He had committed to coaching this team, and he would do his very best. We absolutely loved it!

The team showed steady improvement, and even those teammates we considered less athletic began to flourish. To this day, I still get notes from some of them, reminiscing about the best summer baseball experience we ever had.

Striving for excellence and helping others do the same, developing our gifts and talents to the full is something we are made for. Jesus explained his mission in this world: "I came so that they might have life and have it more abundantly" (John 10:10). Without a doubt, part of that abundant life is the flourishing of our natural capacities, both as individuals and as communities. It doesn't stop there. After all, this world is passing away, and the more spiritual values and virtues that develop from within are what will propel us into everlasting life. We are made to live, work, and thrive in every dimension of our human nature.

Striving for excellence was one of ancient Greece's core values. They believed that human greatness consisted in what they called *arete*. This referred to excellence in any form, to the human value of striving for and achieving greatness in any endeavor, from the moral to the artistic to the athletic. This is the one pagan value that St. Paul includes in his famous list of what we should set our minds on:

> Finally, brothers, whatever is true, whatever is honorable, whatever is just, whatever is pure, whatever is lovely, whatever is gracious, if there is any excellence and if there is anything worthy of praise, think about these things (Philippians 4:8).

All the terms in that inspiring list appear throughout the Bible—they are part of the Judeo-Christian heritage—except the word *excellence*. That is an explicit nod to this human instinct that even the pagans recognized and lauded.

As Christians, we should have our hearts in heaven but our feet firmly on the ground. We are pilgrims making our way toward our eternal home, but our progress depends on giving our best here and now. We don't strive for moral and human excellence to become worthy of God's love or to earn our way into heaven. That's impossible. God's love is unconditional and just needs to be humbly accepted. Nothing we could ever do would earn the surpassing gift of eternal life in Christ—that, too, is a free and joyful gift from the Lord.

Our eagerness to do good and to develop our soul and the world around us flows from the joy of being alive and being given the power of creativity by God. We are made to be builders of great things, from cultures to relationships. When we do what we are created to do with excellence, we help fill the world with light, happiness, and beauty.

Making It Your Own

† Choose one sentence from this chapter that really resonated in your heart or compose a one-sentence summary. Write it on a sticky note. Put it where you will see it throughout the week as a reminder that striving for excellence is part of our human vocation.

† Take time this week to reflect prayerfully on your past experiences of striving for excellence. When have you felt the satisfaction of a job well done? When have you felt the disappointment of not giving your all? What factors contributed to those experiences?

† Sometime this week, write down what motivates you. Are you happy with those motivations? Are they pure and free, or are they stained with fears or self-centeredness? After reflecting on the actual motivations at work in your life, reflect on the motivations that you would like to be more prevalent. How can you feed those good ones and starve the others?

† This week, take time doing an activity that corresponds to some of your natural talents that you don't normally exercise. Give yourself permission to enjoy them, trusting that God takes joy in them, too.

† Think about someone in your life who seems to be discouraged or frustrated. Reach out to encourage that person this week. Find a way to remind her or him of his or her value, regardless of any achievements or failures. Help him or her find a creative way to make a fresh start.

Chapter 10: *Peace*

Do you consider summer to be a peaceful season? Peacefulness is probably not the first thing that comes to mind when you think about summer. But maybe that has more to do with your understanding of peace than it does with your understanding of the values of summer.

We usually associate peace with a lack of conflict or turbulence. And that's true, as far as it goes. But the biblical view of peace is much richer. It begins with a lack of conflict, but it includes the consequences of those circumstances. When conflict and injustice are absent from a human community, then that community is free to flourish. People can work and play without fear. This means they enjoy the blessings of prosperity and social harmony. All of those values are included in the biblical concept of peace.

In that sense, summer is a season of peace. It is a time of growth and plenty, a time of bustling and joyful activity that fills life with gusto. That's a vision we can all appreciate and pursue.

Summer teaches us that side of peace. It can teach us about the joyful side of work. Working and building a personal life and a family life are privileges and joys. Having the freedom and opportunity to engage in that kind of work is a sign and fruit of peace, of a society that is well-ordered and well-protected. Often we forget this side of work, its intrinsic dignity and value. We focus so much on finishing the job or on getting the paycheck that we lose our capacity to enjoy the actual process of working and building, a process we are meant to enjoy. The feeling of interior satisfaction that comes at the end of a hard, honest day of work is a kind of peace within our reach in a special way during the ordinary days of summer, when the sun burns hot and the daylight lasts long.

The household I grew up in, like many others, was marked by a lot of conflict. Tempers flared frequently. My parents separated and divorced when I was young, and that instability increased tensions and violent outbursts. For many years, my home was a place to live, but I didn't feel it was a place to flourish. I felt I had to maneuver carefully in order to avoid stepping on land mines or stirring up machine-gun nests.

One way I coped with this was escaping. I loved to spend weekends sleeping over at friends' houses, especially friends whose parents were still together. I also cultivated a passion for reading. I devoured fiction of all kinds. I always had a book close at hand, and I was always looking for a safe corner to curl up in and disappear into a world where conflicts ended up being resolved and peace was always somehow restored.

It took me a long time to transition out of those coping mechanisms. For years I believed, at least subconsciously, that the fictional dramas I loved so dearly outlined the true path to personal fulfillment and happiness. I tried to imitate the extraordinary adventures of books instead of learning to enjoy and nourish my soul on the ordinary realities of human life. I couldn't find beauty and meaning in ordinary things. I couldn't find peace in the present moment. My escapism led me down plenty of dangerous paths. And although the Lord protected me more than I deserved, I didn't travel them completely unscathed.

One aspect of the life of Jesus Christ surprises and strikes me as much now as it did the first time I thought about it. It has to do with what theologians and spiritual writers traditionally call his "hidden life."

Jesus began his public career as a preacher and miracle worker when he was about thirty years old. That is the part of his life most familiar to us. We all remember the dramatic events that surrounded his birth, but what about the years between his infancy and his public life? What about those thirty years when he lived a normal, working-class life with Mary and Joseph in the small town of Nazareth? Why did the Son of God spend the vast majority of his time on earth in such normalcy and obscurity?

One interpretation might be that he wanted to show us that the most important things in life are the normal things. The primary arena of spiritual development and growth in happiness is the arena of daily life. Hard work, family interactions, and social engagement may not always seem romantic and dramatic in the Hollywood sense, but that's the rich, natural soil where the human heart finds what it needs to grow.

Our fallen nature tends to disrupt the peaceful rhythms of daily living. Sin and selfishness intrude and stir up conflict and turbulence. Lies, laziness, arrogance, and greed—the enemies of the simple abundance and prosperity—disrupt whatever natural peace we find. Our divided hearts spark divisions and conflicts uprooting the very love that is supposed to give meaning to our lives. Here is how St. James describes it:

> Where do the wars and where do the conflicts among you come from? Is it not from your passions that make war within your members?....For where jealousy and selfish ambition exist, there is disorder and every foul practice. But the wisdom from above is first of

all pure, then peaceable, gentle, compliant, full
of mercy and good fruits, without inconstancy
or insincerity. And the fruit of righteousness
is sown in peace for those who cultivate peace
(James 4:1, 3:16–18).

We will never have perfect peace in this life—that's
reserved for heaven. But if we give God the place
he should have in our hearts, we can grow in the
peace that he wants for us. Jesus told his apostles:
"Peace I leave with you; my peace I give to you.
Not as the world gives do I give it to you. Do not
let your hearts be troubled or afraid" (John 14:27).
To experience the "peace of God that surpasses all
understanding" (Philippians 4:7), we have to follow
the teachings and example of the Prince of Peace,
of Jesus himself.

We have to learn to value and accept Nazareth—
the simple things of life—as much as he did. We
have to become peacemakers ourselves, making
kindness and mercy into the default settings of
our heart and mind and to "have no anxiety at
all, but in everything, by prayer and petition, with
thanksgiving" make our requests, needs, hopes,
and problems known to God. If we do, then "the
God of peace will be with" us (Philippians 4:6, 9),
and our daily life will take on more and more of the
summerlike gusto that it's supposed to have.

Making It Your Own

✝ Choose one sentence from this chapter that really resonated in your heart or compose a one-sentence summary. Write it on a sticky note. Put it where you will see it throughout the week as a reminder to look for peace in the flow of ordinary life events.

✝ Spend time this week prayerfully reflecting on Nazareth. Use your imagination to picture the daily life of Jesus, Mary, and Joseph. Think about what God wants to teach you through his coming to earth and spending thirty years in quiet, ordinary obscurity. Dialogue in prayer with Jesus, Mary, and Joseph about their experience. Write down your conclusions.

✝ What factors are inhibiting you from experiencing the fruitfulness and joy of peace? Write them down. Go through each of them and ask yourself what, if anything, you can do about them. Commit to doing at least one of those things this week.

✝ Who in your circle of friends and relatives would you consider to be a peacemaker? Why? What aspects of their behavior do you find attractive? What can you do to learn from them and improve your own ability to be a peacemaker?

† Get together this week with a friend or a mentor and ask the person to talk with you about the conflicts in your life. Invite your friend or mentor to ask tough questions and share his or her honest opinion about how you may be contributing to those conflicts. With that person's help, try to identify patterns in your thinking or behavior that you could adjust to eliminate useless conflicts.

Chapter 11: *Determination*

Summer heat waves make life uncomfortable. They drain your energy and empty your reserve supply of motivation—especially if they coincide with jobs that require sustained effort or repetitive actions. Summer is a lovely season with plenty of benefits, but its weeks of scorching heat and suffocating humidity put our determination to the test.

Increased heat is necessary for the growth meant to happen during summer in both the plant and animal kingdoms. The stronger sunlight, the increased humidity, and the warmer temperatures create an environment that helps growth. In other words, nature brings on the heat for a reason. It isn't an inconvenient obstacle but a required condition for expansion in the natural world, regardless of how uncomfortable it may make us feel.

That kind of discomfort, in fact, has a similar purpose in our own spiritual expansion. Working through difficulties and challenges with determination can lead to spiritual growth, just as exposure to the summer sun is required for growing a bumper crop of wheat, barley, or corn.

As a priest, I frequently encounter people suffering from a lack of determination. It's easy to make a good decision in a moment of light and grace, but somewhere along the way to completion the initial good feelings and clarity wane. A heat wave comes and drains our energy. We begin to second-guess our decision because it is proving to be tougher than we thought or we just don't feel like persevering. So we change course instead of following through. When this becomes a habitual pattern, we never really mature, and our lives begin to lose zest and vigor. Underneath the surface, we constantly feel like an adolescent in a bad mood.

This lack of follow-through takes many forms. Just think about the typical New Year's resolution. A week into January and it's already forgotten. Think about the good ideas we take away from a retreat or a beautiful confession. So often they barely make it out of the realm of ideas. We want to pray every day, but we just can't seem to get started. We want to spend more quality time with our spouse or kids, but the schedule just never seems to ease up. We want to stop wasting so much time on video games or social media or gossip, but the right time to start never really comes around.

This can also happen with more substantial dimensions of our life. Every marriage goes through trials, real heat waves where all the joy and consolation seem to be used up. Persevering through those seasons leads to greater intimacy and a whole new experience of joy, but many couples never get that far because their determination is undermined. Priests and members of religious orders find that their initial zeal wanes after a season or two of ministry, and they begin to question whether or not they were truly called to their consecration. They mistake the normal problems of life—the uncomfortable and sometimes excruciating heat waves of high summer—for an indication that they have chosen the wrong path.

One of my early attempts at a summer job was cutting grass. A neighbor down the road had a small front lawn. He lived alone and he was out of town a lot. I wanted to make some money, and he hired me to cut his grass.

The problem was that I hated yard work. I could shelve books in a library for ten hours a day, but after a mere ten minutes working in the yard I would be struck by my own personal heat wave. But this yard was small and close to home, and I wanted to earn some money, so I figured it would be OK.

I cut it once, and everything was fine. Then my neighbor went out of town again. He was going to be gone for a month, so I relaxed. No rush. I could cut it any time. A week passed, and the grass was growing. Then another week, and the grass kept growing. I kept making excuses to put off my duty. About halfway through the third week this guy's yard was beginning to look like an African savannah. The grass was knee high, patchy, and thoroughly unkempt. My conscience was weighing me down, but I was stuck in my heat wave. I just didn't have the willpower to do what I had committed to do. Every time I passed by the yard I grimaced. But I consoled myself by remembering I still had some time before my neighbor would get home. Then he came back—early.

He called my house and demanded that I come give him an explanation. I made my way over, stricken with guilt. He greeted me and took me on a tour of his front field. He was *not* pleased. He was *not* going to pay me for anything. I was fired.

Fired?! That was humiliating. And shameful. It was entirely my fault. I had no excuses, except that I had taken on a commitment—a reasonable one—and I simply didn't follow through with it. For no other reason than I didn't feel like it. My dad would never have done that. My older sister would never have done that. Everyone I admired would never have done that. I had simply failed in my duty without even trying.

The experience sparked some self-reflection. I don't remember if I made any specific resolution, but I do remember that I thoroughly detested feeling the way I felt. The memory of that feeling became a motivation in the future. I thought more carefully about my decisions and commitments, and I was able to fulfill unpleasant duties with greater consistency.

Jesus talked about this in one his most famous parables, the parable of the Sower. It's the story of a farmer who went out to plant his seed. Some seed fell on the hard path, and the birds came and ate it up. Some seed fell on good soil, but when it started to grow some nearby thorn bushes choked it. Some seed fell on good soil and produced an abundant crop, and some seed fell on shallow, rocky soil. These last seeds started to grow exuberantly. They sprang up quickly and showed remarkable promise. But then a heat wave came, and their shallow roots couldn't penetrate the rocky soil deeply enough to find moisture. As a result, the plants withered and died. Here is how Jesus explains the image:

> The seed sown on rocky ground is the one who hears the word and receives it at once with joy. But he has no root and lasts only for a time. When some tribulation or persecution comes because of the word, he immediately falls away (Matthew 13:20–21).

Making a good decision is only the first step. We have to follow through with it, to persevere, to exercise the determination necessary to allow that decision to produce its promised good results, regardless of heat waves, 100 percent humidity, and any other difficulty or obstacle that presents itself.

The best way to develop healthy determination is to take time to reflect on our motives. In perfect weather, we need to make sure that our decisions are flowing from wise principles and authentic values, not whims or fashions. When the heat wave comes—and it will come—we need to admit the adverse feelings it stirs up and distinguish those temporary sentiments from the perennial principles and values that are at the heart of our motivations and decisions. Those are deeper than our fickle feelings. The more we intentionally live from the deeper level, the stronger we become. That's what growing up is all about.

Making It Your Own

† Choose one sentence from this chapter that really resonated in your heart or compose a one-sentence summary. Write it on a sticky note. Put it where you will see it throughout the week as a reminder of the importance of determination.

† Take time this week to examine prayerfully your level of determination. Where do you regularly tend to fall short? What decisions have you made multiple times but been unable to carry out? Why? Is the decision itself flawed or is your determination too weak? Write down the answers to these questions so you can reach a greater degree of clarity.

† This week, become cognizant of the decisions you make and how thoroughly you follow through. Pay attention to which decisions are hard to make and why. What is the root of your indecisiveness? Pay attention to the small decisions you make and follow through with them consciously (like the decision to take a coffee break, to skip lunch in order to get more work done, and so on). Every day you are making dozens of decisions. If you want them to be in greater harmony with your core values, you have to be aware of them.

† Have you ever had to work with someone who couldn't finish the job? How did that make you feel? How did it affect your own efforts or the efforts of those around you? How did you react? What can you do this week to become the kind of person who always finishes the job?

† Do you remember the old fable about the tortoise and the hare? They were in a race where the hare started out fast but got distracted and went off the path. The tortoise started off slowly and kept up that pace. In the end, his constancy and determination won him the race. In which situations of life are you more like the tortoise? In which situations are you more like the hare? Why?

Chapter 12: *Forgiveness*

Summer is a season of recovery. The other seasons tend to be harsh and violent; they can cause a lot of damage. Trees lose limbs or collapse under the weight of ice and snow; high winds tear them apart; frost kills their buds. Summertime, however, always seems to find a way to make up for those losses. The long period of warmth and light releases fresh energy and renewed vitality. It allows new growth patterns to transform old wounds into unique, beautiful features.

Our lives are like that. We are wounded multiple times as we make our way through this earthly pilgrimage. Tragedies arrive uninvited and tear away hopes or relationships we thought we could not live without. Loved ones abandon or betray us. Expectations rise only to be shattered again and again. And yet God's grace can always find a way into those wounds, giving us a season of new growth, reshaping us in unforeseen and beautiful ways. We just need to be open to change, strong enough to forgive and release whatever needs to be forgiven and released, while staying flexible enough not to break under the strain.

After my family had gone through two divorces and the death of my mother, I had a void in my life. I was like a tree that lost an important limb in a winter storm. But my roots were still intact, and the trunk still wanted to grow. God provided new influences to help that happen. One of them was Mrs. McBride.

She was my sixth-grade English teacher. I remember her as being very proper and very kind. She had the type of personality that made it easy for her to discipline the class. In fact, it seemed she didn't even have to discipline us. Her mere presence was enough to keep us attentive and in line. She was also a gifted teacher who loved the English language and teaching us about it.

That year we learned how to diagram sentences on the blackboard. I just loved it. But my assigned seat was in the back of the classroom, and I must have been squinting a lot. She noticed and sent me to get my eyesight checked out. I needed glasses. It was nice that someone had noticed and helped me solve that problem, a problem I didn't even know I had. It was a motherly thing to do.

As the year went on, Mrs. McBride noticed my interest in English and continued to encourage me. She let me stay after school to spend more time on my compositions. She gave me personal feedback. She always seemed to have a kind word and a smile for me whenever we would run into each other in the hallway. The harder I worked, the more feedback she gave me, the more encouragement, the more guidance.

I don't know if she was aware of my family situation, but she always gave me just the right amount of nurturing. She never tried to be for me what she couldn't be (another mom, for instance). But she was for me—and for all of us—what she was called to be: our teacher. Her influence helped me find a constructive outlet not only for my youthful energies but for my natural talents and even for my emotions. Reading and writing became a powerful mode of processing what I was feeling and going through. Mrs. McBride's wise dedication to her students was one way God's providence found of bringing new life and a new pattern of growth to a young tree that was wounded but filled with life.

That's how it always is with God. The wounds, the losses, the betrayals, the tragedies—they never have to be the last word. We just have to accept them and release them, name them and forgive them. Then they can become opportunities for new growth. This is the meaning of redemption. God didn't save the world after evil defaced it by throwing it away and starting over. He took the fallen and wounded world and poured his grace into it. Jesus didn't come to destroy, but to renew, to recover, and to redeem:

> For God so loved the world that he gave his only Son, so that everyone who believes in him might not perish but might have eternal life. For God did not send his Son into the world to condemn the world, but that the world might be saved through him (John 3:16-17).

A forgiving heart, a heart that can let go of offenses and betrayals, is a heart that opens itself to God's redeeming grace. It allows God's providence to provide a summer season, a season of warmth and light that can heal what needs to be healed and spur a new and glorious pattern of growth. The next time you see a twisted tree trunk or a damaged landscape, look for the beauty that nature brought out of the brokenness and allow it to echo in your hearts by saying the silent prayer, "I forgive…." You can rest assured that God, ever faithful, will know exactly when and how to send you Mrs. McBride.

Making It Your Own

† Choose one sentence from this chapter that really resonated in your heart or compose a one-sentence summary. Write it on a sticky note. Put it where you will see it throughout the week as a reminder that a forgiving heart is a heart open to new life and new beauty.

† Take time this week to prayerfully reflect on the "Mrs. McBrides" God has sent into your life. Savor the good memories and pray a prayer of thanksgiving to God for them.

† This week, take a walk through the woods. Take your time. Notice the hidden drama of growth all around you. Look for signs of wounds and how the vital power of nature responded to them. Appreciate the beauty of the solutions that providence provided and continues to give.

† Reflect on your responsibilities in life. Are you living them to the fullest? Are you pouring yourself into them with gusto, as Mrs. McBride did, or are you just going through the motions? What can you do this week to jump-start a more intentional and fulfilling engagement in your normal life duties?

† Take time this week to visit your parish church, or a parish close to where you work, when nothing special is going on. Look around the church for all the religious images and symbols. Find the saints and decorations and learn the stories behind them. Reflect on how each one of them embodies the rhythm of redemption. Allow this message of Christ's redemption to open your heart and help you release any resentment, fear, or discouragement lingering there.

The author, **Fr. John Bartunek, LC, SThD**, splits his time between Michigan, where he continues his writing apostolate and assists at Our Lady Queen of the Family Retreat Center in Oxford, and Rome, where he teaches theology at the Pontifical Athenaeum Regina Apostolorum. He is the author of several books, including *The Better Part* and *Inside the Passion: An Insider's Look at the Passion of the Christ.* Fr. Bartunek became a member of the Catholic Church in 1991, was ordained a Catholic priest in 2003, and earned his doctorate in moral theology in 2010. His online retreats are available at **RCSpirituality.org**, and he answers questions about the spiritual life at **SpiritualDirection.com**.

CPSIA information can be obtained
at www.ICGtesting.com
Printed in the USA
LVHW091327020619
619667LV00008B/13/P

9 780764 825620